Earn from Web Development

Rajamanickam Antonimuthu

Introduction

In this book, I invite you to embark on a journey alongside me as I share my personal experiences in transforming web development skills into a rewarding source of income. I already shared some details as part of my previous Book "Emerging Technologies for Profit". In this book, I am going to give more details specific to web development. Here, you'll find not just theoretical knowledge, but a roadmap paved with my own footsteps, guiding you from acquiring essential skills to navigating the landscape of monetization.

Whether you're a budding developer eager to turn passion into profit or a seasoned professional seeking to refine your strategies, this book offers valuable insights gleaned from the trenches of real-world experience. Get ready to dive into the intricacies of coding your way to financial success, armed with proven tactics and actionable advice. Prepare to unlock the potential of web development not just as a technical skill, but as a powerful tool for forging a fulfilling and financially independent future. Note that this book is NOT a tutorial for teaching web development, but it is for sharing my experiences and discussing web development. As you can find a lot of free tutorial websites (e.g.w3schools.com) and free detailed tutorial videos provided by many YouTube channels (e.g freeCodeCamp), I am NOT including any tutorial here.

I'm excited to share my journey with you. Let's explore the exciting world of web development, where lines of code blossom into tangible rewards, and technical expertise translates into a life transformed. If you're interested, you can hire me for affordable hourly charges to receive one-on-one coaching on doing online business.

Why Web Development? Understanding the Earning Potential:

Are you passionate about web development and eager to turn your skills into a rewarding career? This book is your roadmap to success. Here, you'll find insights gleaned from real-world experience, guiding you through the practical realities of building a lucrative web development practice. There are huge opportunities available with web development if you are willing to spend effective time learning key things of web development, and working sincerely for your customers, clients, or users.

As the saying goes, "*know everything about something and something about everything*," emphasizing the need for a strong foundation in web development fundamentals and deep expertise in a specific technology. Whether you choose PHP, HTML, JavaScript, front-end development, database administration, graphic design, or testing, aim to become an expert in your chosen field.

The journey to mastery involves learning through **rigorous study**, **hands-on practice**, and active **discussion**. Engage in workshops, online forums, and communities to broaden your horizons and refine your skills. Remember, effective communication is key to understanding requirements and delivering optimal results.

The landscape of web development is constantly evolving. Embrace emerging technologies like artificial intelligence, single-page applications, and cloud computing to remain competitive and deliver cutting-edge solutions.

The rise of the internet has connected the world, and people increasingly rely on online platforms for information, communication, and commerce. Web development thrives on this growing demand for convenience and accessibility.

At the heart of every successful web project lies the user. Your applications should prioritize user experience through intuitive navigation, clear messaging, visually appealing design, and seamless performance. This applies whether you're building for large corporations, freelancing for diverse clients, or launching your own web-based business.

My experience as a web developer encompasses working for major corporations, freelancing on numerous projects, and developing and selling web applications like the Web Timesheet software. I've worn many hats, and this book distills the lessons learned into actionable advice for your success.

If you're transitioning from desktop applications to web development, remember that websites operate on stateless protocols. Each interaction, like typing a URL, is a separate request-response cycle. For example, when you type the website URL "QualityPointTech.Com" into the address bar of the browser, you are asking the web server to send the content of QualityPointTech.Com's home page. You will see that content on your browser screen once the server responds with the output for your request. Both are independent events. Keep this fundamental principle in mind when building web applications.

Begin your journey with the basics. Learn HTML to create simple static web pages. Introduce Javascript to add interactivity, and then utilize CSS to elevate the visual appeal. Next, delve into server-side languages like PHP and databases with SQL to become a well-rounded full-stack developer. Remember, consistent practice is key to solidifying your understanding.

I encourage you to explore the world of web development with curiosity and dedication. As your skills flourish and your expertise deepens, you'll unlock the doors to a fulfilling and financially rewarding career. Let's embark on this journey together! Various statistics project good growth potential for web developers from both the revenue perspective as well as opportunities perspective.

Companies like Amazon, eBay, and Alibaba initially operated solely as online retailers, leveraging websites as their primary sales and interaction channel. Facebook, Google, and Twitter primarily started as web-based platforms to fulfill specific digital needs, gradually expanding their functionalities and evolving into major corporations. Many successful companies today have adopted and integrated online presence into their operations.

Web Development Journey

The internet is a vast digital landscape, filled with websites of all shapes and sizes. But behind every stunning interface and engaging experience lies the invisible hand of the web developer. If you're drawn to the allure of crafting websites and shaping the online world, then embarking on a web development journey is a thrilling prospect. But where do you begin? Fear not, aspiring coder! This guide will equip you with the tools and knowledge to navigate your path to web development mastery.

Laying the Foundation:

- Building Blocks of Code: Start with the fundamentals – HTML, CSS, and Javascript. These are the building blocks of every website, and like any language, mastering them unlocks the potential to express yourself creatively. Online tutorials, coding camps, and online forums are invaluable companions.
- Practice Makes Perfect: Don't get intimidated by lines of code. Practice makes perfect, so grab a text editor and start building simple projects. Experiment, tinker, and embrace the occasional error – it's all part of the learning process.

Expanding Your Horizons:

- Dive into Frameworks: Once you've grasped the basics, explore frameworks like React or Vue.js. These frameworks provide pre-built components and structures, accelerating your development and creating stunning, interactive websites.
- Backend Power: While front-end development shapes the user experience, the backend is the engine that drives it. Learn server-side languages like Python or PHP to understand how websites interact with databases and process information.
- Beyond the Code: Web development isn't just about code. Master version control tools like Git to manage your projects and collaborate with others. Learn about web accessibility and user experience (UX) design to ensure your creations are inclusive and user-friendly. Learn about performance, SEO, and responsive design.

Fueling Your Journey:

- Community Matters: Surround yourself with fellow developers! Online forums, meetups, and communities offer invaluable support, advice, and inspiration.
- Never Stop Learning: The web development landscape is constantly evolving, so embrace continuous learning. Attend workshops, read industry blogs, and explore new technologies.
- Build Your Portfolio: Showcase your skills! Create personal projects, contribute to open-source initiatives, and build a portfolio that demonstrates your creativity and technical abilities.

Remember, the road to web development mastery is a marathon, not a sprint. Be patient, persistent, and passionate. Celebrate your victories, learn from your mistakes, and most importantly, have fun! The web awaits your unique voice and creative vision. So, grab your keyboard, code like a champion, and build the digital future you dream of.

Bonus Tips:

- Find a mentor: Seek guidance from experienced developers who can answer your questions and provide valuable insights.
- Contribute to open-source projects: Get real-world experience and collaborate with others while learning from their code.
- Attend hackathons and coding challenges: Test your skills, network with other developers, and push yourself to create innovative solutions.

With dedication and a dash of digital wizardry, you can transform your passion for web development into a fulfilling and rewarding career. Go forth, code conquerer, and build your digital legacy!

Basics of Internet

Embarking on a journey into web development is akin to setting sail into the vast ocean of the internet. Understanding the foundational elements of this digital realm is crucial for aspiring web developers. In this guide, we'll unravel the basics of the internet, providing you with a compass to navigate and thrive in the dynamic world of web development.

1. The Internet: A Global Network:

At its core, the Internet is a global network of interconnected computers. This network facilitates the seamless exchange of information, allowing users to connect, share, and access data from virtually anywhere in the world.

2. Protocols and Standards:

Protocols and standards serve as the language of the internet, ensuring that devices communicate effectively. HTTP (Hypertext Transfer Protocol) and HTTPS (Hypertext Transfer Protocol Secure) govern web communication, while HTML (Hypertext Markup Language) structures content, and CSS (Cascading Style Sheets) styles the presentation.

3. Domains and URLs:

Domains are human-readable addresses that point to specific locations on the internet. URLs (Uniform Resource Locators) act as the navigation system, providing the precise location of web resources. Understanding the anatomy of a URL is fundamental for web developers.

Each domain consists of a top-level domain (TLD) and a second-level domain (SLD), such as ".com" and "example" in "example.com." TLDs vary from generic (.com, .org) to country-specific (.us, .uk).

Uniform Resource Locators (URLs) act as the coordinates on our web journey. Comprising several components, they specify the protocol (HTTP or HTTPS), the domain (www.example.com), the path (/resources/page), query parameters (?id=123), and fragments (#section). This structured format is our guide through the intricate web of information.

Securing a domain involves registering it through a domain registrar. Think of registrars like the custodians of your chosen storefront sign, where you renew ownership annually to retain control. Popular registrars, such as GoDaddy or Namecheap, facilitate this process, allowing you to claim your unique space in the digital city.

The Domain Name System (DNS) acts as the translator of our human-readable domains into machine-readable IP addresses. It operates in a hierarchical structure, with authoritative name servers distributing the responsibility of translating domain names into numerical identifiers. DNS ensures a seamless connection between users and web servers.

Subdomains are like specialized sections within a store. They allow for the organization and structuring of content. For instance, in "blog.example.com," "blog" serves as a subdomain of "example.com," offering a dedicated space for blog-related content.

URL encoding becomes crucial when special characters enter the scene. It's the method of representing these characters to ensure proper transmission and interpretation by browsers and servers. Spaces become "%20," and symbols like "&" transform into "%26," ensuring smooth communication in the complex web landscape.

In the evolving landscape of internet security, HTTPS (Hypertext Transfer Protocol Secure) has become paramount. It encrypts data during transmission, providing a secure layer for sensitive information. Users can identify secure connections by the presence of a padlock icon in their browsers.

4. Web Browsers: Gateways to the Internet:

Web browsers are the portals through which users access the internet. Popular browsers like Chrome, Firefox, and Safari interpret HTML, CSS, and JavaScript to render web pages. As a web developer, familiarity with multiple browsers ensures compatibility and a consistent user experience.

5. HTML: The Backbone of the Web:

HTML, or Hypertext Markup Language, is the fundamental building block of web pages. It structures content through tags, defining elements such as headings, paragraphs, and images. A solid grasp of HTML is essential for any web developer.

6. CSS: Styling the Web:

Cascading Style Sheets (CSS) bring aesthetics to web development. By styling HTML elements, CSS enables developers to create visually appealing and responsive designs. Understanding selectors, properties, and the box model is key to effective styling.

7. JavaScript: Bringing Interactivity to the Web:

JavaScript is the scripting language that adds interactivity to web pages. Aspiring web developers should delve into JavaScript to create dynamic and responsive user interfaces, handle events, and manipulate the Document Object Model (DOM).

8. Servers and Hosting:

Web development involves not only creating content but also hosting it. Servers store website files and deliver them to users upon request. Learning about server architecture, hosting providers, and server-side languages (e.g., Node.js, PHP) is crucial for a comprehensive understanding.

Embarking on the path of web development is an exhilarating journey through the vast expanse of the internet. As you grasp the basics of protocols, coding languages, and collaborative tools, you'll find yourself equipped to not only navigate but also shape the digital landscape. Stay curious, embrace the learning process, and let your journey into web development be an exciting exploration of endless possibilities. Happy coding!

How to earn from Web Development?

You can monetize your web development skills in various ways. You need not be an expert to start earning money. Even with very little HTML knowledge, you will be able to earn money by doing simple HTML markup works or even developing simple static websites for small businesses.
The world of web development offers exciting avenues for earning while doing what you love. Here are some ways you can turn your coding skills into income:

Freelancing:

- Platforms: Sign up on freelance platforms like Upwork, Fiverr, or Freelancer.com to connect with clients seeking web development services. Offer your skills in specific areas like front-end development, back-end development, or full-stack development. Begin with smaller projects to build your reputation, gather positive reviews, and gradually increase your rates as you gain experience.
- Direct contracts: Build your network and pitch your services directly to businesses or individuals needing website development, maintenance, or custom solutions.

Offer Maintenance and Support Services:

- Provide ongoing maintenance and support services for websites. Many clients are willing to pay for regular updates, bug fixes, and improvements. This not only ensures a steady income but also builds long-term relationships with clients.

Employment:

- Full-time jobs: Apply for web developer positions at tech companies, agencies, or startups. Look for job boards like Indeed, Glassdoor, or LinkedIn to find suitable opportunities.
- Contract work: Consider shorter-term contract work with companies needing developers for specific projects. This can offer flexibility and variety.

Building your own products:

- Develop and sell web applications: Create software tools, productivity apps, or niche solutions that cater to specific needs and sell them online.
- Create and monetize websites: Build content-based websites, e-commerce sites, or membership platforms and generate revenue through ads, subscriptions, or product sales.
- Develop Custom Themes and Plugins. For those proficient in platforms like WordPress, consider creating custom themes or plugins. Sell them on marketplaces like ThemeForest or CodeCanyon. This allows you to earn passive income as users purchase your products.

Teaching and consulting:

- Online courses: Share your knowledge by creating and selling online courses on platforms like Udemy, Skillshare, or Coursera.
- Coding bootcamps: Teach web development skills at coding bootcamps or workshops, catering to beginner, intermediate, or advanced learners.

- Consulting services: Offer consulting services to businesses or individuals, helping them with website strategy, development best practices, or technical troubleshooting.

Additional income streams:

- Affiliate marketing: Promote other web development tools, products, or services and earn commissions on referrals.
- Bug bounties: Contribute to open-source projects or participate in bug bounty programs to earn rewards for identifying and fixing vulnerabilities.
- Speaking engagements: Share your expertise at conferences, meetups, or online events for speaking fees.

Remember:

- Build your portfolio: Showcase your skills and past projects to attract clients or employers.
- Network actively: Connect with other developers, attend industry events, and build your professional reputation.
- Stay updated: Continuously learn and adapt to new technologies and trends to remain competitive in the market.

The key to earning from web development lies in identifying your skillset, choosing the right path, and continuously honing your craft. With dedication and creativity, you can turn your coding passion into a rewarding and lucrative career.

Best Practices in Web Development

Responsive Design:

Ensure your websites are designed to be responsive, providing an optimal viewing experience across a variety of devices and screen sizes. Responsive design is like magic for your website - it makes it automatically adjust to look and function perfectly on any screen, from massive desktop monitors to tiny smartphone screens. Imagine one website that magically transforms itself to fit seamlessly in any hand, pocket, or desk!

Why Responsive Design Matters:

- More People, More Screens: These days, people access the internet through all sorts of devices - phones, tablets, laptops, you name it. Responsive design ensures your website looks great and works well on all of them, no matter the size or resolution.

- Happy Users, Happy Business: No one likes squinting at tiny text or scrolling sideways forever. A responsive website keeps users happy and engaged, which means more sales, leads, or whatever your website goals are.
- Google Loves It: Search engines like Google love websites that cater to all devices. Having a responsive design can boost your search ranking, bringing more visitors to your digital doorstep.

How Responsive Design Works:

- Flexible Layouts: Think of your website's layout as a rubber band, stretching and adapting to fit different screen sizes. Images resize, text reflows, and buttons move around to create the best possible experience on each device.
- Media Queries: These are like secret instructions whispered to the website, telling it how to behave on different screen sizes. "If the screen is small, make the menu button bigger!" or "If the screen is wide, show two columns of content instead of one."
- Benefits Galore: A responsive website saves you time and money by eliminating the need to create separate versions for different devices. It also improves user experience, search engine ranking, and ultimately, your website's success.

Getting Started with Responsive Design:

- Choose a Responsive Theme: Many website builders and content management systems come with built-in responsive themes. Choose one that suits your style and start customizing.
- Learn the Basics: There are plenty of free resources online to teach you the basics of responsive design. Don't worry, you don't need to be a coding wizard!
- Test and Tweak: Once you've built your responsive website, test it on different devices and browsers to make sure everything looks and works as it should. Fine-tune it until it's perfect!

Remember, responsive design isn't just a trend, it's the future of web development. By making your website accessible and enjoyable on all screens, you're reaching a wider audience and setting yourself up for success in the ever-evolving digital world. So, grab your magic wand (or coding keyboard) and start building responsive websites that enchant users on every device!

Mobile-First Approach:

Design and develop with mobile devices in mind first, then progressively enhance for larger screens. This ensures a seamless experience on all devices.
The Mobile-First Approach is a web design philosophy that flips the script. Instead of starting with desktops and shrinking things down for phones, it begins with creating the perfect experience for small screens and then expands upon it for larger devices. Think

of it like crafting a tiny, intricate masterpiece of a website, then carefully blowing it up like a magical bubble, ensuring every detail remains flawless and captivating.

Here's why Mobile-First wins:

Real World Reflects Mobile: Most people access the internet through their phones these days. Starting with mobile ensures your website shines where it's used most.

Prioritize Essentials: Small screens force you to focus on the core content and functionality, making your website clear, concise, and engaging for everyone.

Efficiency Boosts: Building from mobile up is often faster and more efficient than adapting large designs for smaller screens. It's like carving a statue from a single block of wood, rather than piecing it together from scraps.

Future-Proofing: As internet use on mobile devices continues to grow, Mobile-First prepares your website for the future. You'll already be ahead of the curve!

How it Works:

- Think Small First: Design the layout, navigation, and content specifically for phone screens. Make sure everything is accessible and user-friendly within thumb's reach.
- Progressive Enhancement: Once the mobile foundation is solid, gradually add features and complexity for larger screens, like tablets and desktops. Think of it as adding layers to your magic bubble, enhancing the experience without losing the core.
- Benefits Galore: Mobile-First websites load faster, use less data, and are generally more user-friendly. They also tend to score higher with search engines, reaching a wider audience.

Making the Switch:

- Mobile-First Tools: Many website builders and frameworks now offer built-in Mobile-First tools and templates. Take advantage of these resources to make the process smooth.
- Start Small: Don't try to rebuild your entire website overnight. Focus on key pages and user flows first, then gradually bring everything else into the Mobile-First fold.
- Embrace the Change: It might feel different at first, but Mobile-First is the way of the future. Embrace the challenge and you'll create websites that truly shine in the palm of your hand!

Remember, Mobile-First isn't just about designing for phones; it's about prioritizing the user experience in today's mobile-first world. By adopting this approach, you'll create websites that are accessible, engaging, and future-proof, leaving a lasting impression on users no matter what device they use. So, shrink down your mindset, expand your creativity, and start building magical mobile-first experiences that captivate every screen!

Cross-Browser Compatibility:

Test your websites on multiple browsers (Chrome, Firefox, Safari, Edge) to ensure consistent functionality and appearance for all users. Cross-browser compatibility sounds fancy, but it's simply ensuring your website works perfectly across different browsers and devices (phones, tablets, desktops).

Why is it important?

- Happy Users, Happy Business: No one likes seeing broken websites or missing features. Cross-browser compatibility keeps users happy and gives them the best possible experience, which leads to more sales, leads, or whatever your website goals are.
- Reach Everyone: Different people use different browsers. By ensuring your website works everywhere, you're not excluding anyone and maximizing your reach.
- SEO Boost: Search engines love websites that work well on all browsers. Having good cross-browser compatibility can help your website rank higher in search results.

How does it work?

- Different Browsers, Different Languages: Think of browsers as speaking different languages. Your website code needs to be able to "speak" to each browser in a way it understands.
- Testing is Key: You can't fix what you don't know! Regularly test your website on different browsers and devices to identify any compatibility issues.
- Tools and Techniques: There are many tools and techniques available to help you achieve cross-browser compatibility. Frameworks like Bootstrap can take care of a lot of the heavy lifting for you.

Getting Started:

- Choose a Modern Framework: Using a modern framework like Bootstrap or Foundation can provide pre-built code that works well across different browsers.
- Validate Your Code: Use online tools like W3C validator to check your code for errors and potential compatibility issues.

- Test Early and Often: Don't wait until the end to test your website. Make it a habit to test on different browsers throughout the development process.

Remember, cross-browser compatibility is an ongoing process. No website is perfect, and new browsers and devices are constantly being released. But by making it a priority and using the right tools, you can ensure your website looks and works its best for everyone, no matter what browser or device they use.

Page Speed Optimization:

Optimize your website's loading speed by minimizing file sizes, leveraging browser caching, and utilizing content delivery networks (CDNs).

Imagine your website as a race car. You put all the bells and whistles in, from stunning visuals to interactive features, but if it takes forever to load, no one will reach the finish line (aka, your content). That's where page speed optimization comes in – it's like tweaking the engine and streamlining the body to make your website a sleek, high-performance machine that rockets users to your content in a flash.

Why is it important?

- Speed Demons Win: Attention spans are shorter than ever, and users expect websites to load in seconds. A speedy website keeps visitors engaged and reduces bounce rates.
- SEO Rocket Fuel: Search engines love fast websites. Optimizing your page speed can boost your search engine ranking, bringing more traffic and potential customers.
- Conversions Take Off: The faster your website loads, the more likely users are to take action, whether it's buying a product, signing up for a newsletter, or contacting you.

How to boost your page speed:

- Image Slimdown: Images can be heavyweights, slowing down your website. Optimize them by compressing their size without compromising quality.
- Minimize Code: Every line of code adds weight. Minify your HTML, CSS, and JavaScript to eliminate unnecessary characters and spaces.
- Caching Champions: Leverage browser caching to store essential files locally on users' devices, so they don't have to download them every time they visit your website.
- Server Sizzle: Choose a reliable web hosting provider with optimized servers to ensure your website runs smoothly even when traffic spikes.
- Lazy Loading: Don't overload users with everything at once. Use lazy loading to only load content as they scroll down the page.

Tools and Techniques:

- Website Speed Testers: Use tools like Google **PageSpeed Insights** or GTmetrix to analyze your website's performance and identify areas for improvement.
- Compression Plugins: Many plugins and tools can automatically optimize your images and code for faster loading.
- CDN Magic: Content delivery networks (CDNs) store your website's content on servers around the world, delivering it to users from the closest location for lightning-fast speeds.

Remember, page speed optimization is an ongoing process. New technologies and tools emerge all the time, so stay informed and keep tweaking your website to maintain its edge.

By prioritizing speed and implementing these tips, you'll transform your website from a sluggish jalopy into a high-performance race car, capturing user attention, boosting conversions, and leaving your mark on the digital highway!

Search Engine Optimization (SEO):

Implement SEO best practices, including proper HTML structure, descriptive tags, and relevant content, to improve visibility on search engines.

Why is SEO important?

- Visibility Matters: No matter how amazing your website is, if no one can find it, it's like whispering secrets to the wind. SEO boosts your visibility in search results, bringing in more visitors and potential customers.
- Organic Traffic Gold: Paid ads are great, but organic traffic (visitors who find you through search) is king. SEO attracts genuine interest, leading to more engaged users and higher conversion rates.
- Long-Term Investment: Unlike paid ads, SEO benefits keep growing over time. The higher you climb in search rankings, the more organic traffic you'll attract, creating a virtuous cycle of success.

How does SEO work?

- Content is King: Search engines love websites with rich, informative content that answers users' queries. Craft content that's relevant, high-quality, and optimized for relevant keywords.
- Keywords like Magic Spells: Keywords are the search terms users type into engines. Sprinkle them strategically throughout your website, but remember, quality content comes first, not keyword stuffing!

- Technical Tweaks: Behind the scenes, your website's structure, code, and mobile-friendliness matter too. Optimize these technical aspects to make your website search engine friendly.
- Backlinks: The Digital Vote: Think of backlinks as online recommendations. The more reputable websites linking to yours, the higher your authority in the eyes of search engines.
- Off-Page Adventures: SEO isn't just about your website. Participate in online communities, guest blog on relevant sites, and build relationships to strengthen your digital presence.

Getting Started with SEO:

- Keyword Research: Identify relevant keywords your target audience is searching for. Tools like Google Keyword Planner can help.
- Content Creation Powerhouse: Craft high-quality content that engages users and answers their questions.
- Technical Tune-Up: Check your website's technical health using tools like Google Search Console and address any issues.
- Link Building Strategy: Focus on building quality backlinks from relevant and authoritative websites.
- Stay Informed: SEO is constantly evolving. Keep up with the latest trends and best practices to maintain your website's visibility.

Remember, SEO is a marathon, not a sprint. Patience, consistent effort, and a focus on user-friendly content are key. By implementing these tips and adapting to the ever-changing landscape, you can guide your website to the top of search results and claim your rightful place among the digital stars.

So, grab your SEO wand, sprinkle on your keyword magic, and build a captivating online presence that shines under the spotlight of search engines!

Security Measures:

Incorporate security practices such as using HTTPS, validating and sanitizing user inputs, and keeping software and plugins up to date to protect against common vulnerabilities.

- Secure Coding Practices: Write secure code from the ground up, following best practices like input validation, SQL injection prevention, and cross-site scripting (XSS) defense. This ensures your code doesn't have vulnerabilities hackers can exploit.
- Strong Authentication and Authorization: Implement robust user authentication with strong passwords, multi-factor authentication (MFA), and role-based access control. This restricts unauthorized access to sensitive data and features. At the

same time, avoid unnecessary complexities if your web application doesn't need them.

- HTTPS and Encryption: Use HTTPS with a valid SSL certificate to encrypt communication between your website and users' browsers. This protects sensitive information like login credentials and credit card details from being intercepted.
- Regular Updates and Patching: Keep your software, plugins, and libraries up-to-date with the latest security patches. This fixes vulnerabilities discovered by developers and security researchers before hackers can exploit them.
- Web Application Firewalls (WAFs): Deploy a WAF to act as a security shield, filtering out malicious traffic and protecting against common web attacks like SQL injection and XSS.
- Security Audits and Penetration Testing: Regularly conduct security audits and penetration testing to identify vulnerabilities in your website and applications. This proactive approach helps you fix security holes before they are exploited.
- Data Backup and Recovery: Implement a reliable data backup and recovery plan to ensure you can quickly restore your website and data in case of a security breach or other disaster.
- Choose a secure web hosting provider with a good reputation for security.

Remember, web security is an ongoing process, not a one-time fix. By implementing these measures and staying vigilant, you can build a secure web presence that protects your users and your data.

Code Modularity and Organization:

Write modular and organized code, following best practices like the separation of concerns, to enhance readability and maintainability.

Imagine a towering skyscraper. Its impressive height wouldn't be possible without a sturdy foundation and well-organized floors, right? Code, in a similar way, thrives on modularity and organization. These principles act as the building blocks of robust and maintainable software.

What is Code Modularity?

Modularity refers to the practice of dividing your code into independent, self-contained units called modules (sometimes referred to as components, classes, or packages, depending on the programming language and paradigm). Each module encapsulates a specific functionality and interacts with other modules through well-defined interfaces.

Think of it like building with LEGO bricks. Each brick represents a module, and you can snap them together in various ways to create complex structures (your software). The key is that each brick (module) is independent and can be easily replaced or modified without affecting the overall structure.

Benefits of Code Modularity:

- Readability and Maintainability: Modular code is easier to understand and maintain. Developers can focus on specific modules without getting bogged down in the entire codebase. This makes it simpler to fix bugs, add new features, and collaborate effectively.
- Reusability: Modules can be reused across different projects or parts of the same project, reducing code duplication and saving development time. Imagine having a pre-built "login module" you can plug into any web application!
- Testability: Smaller, independent modules are easier to test in isolation, leading to more robust and reliable software. You can test each brick of your LEGO castle before assembling the whole thing.
- Scalability: Modular code can be easily scaled to accommodate growing complexity. As your software evolves, you can add or remove modules without major architectural changes.

Organizing Your Code:

Now that we understand the importance of modularity, let's talk about how to organize your code effectively. Here are some key principles:

- Separation of Concerns: Divide your code into modules that handle distinct functionalities, like data access, business logic, and UI rendering. This keeps each module focused and reduces dependencies between them.
- Naming Conventions: Use consistent and meaningful names for your modules, functions, and variables. This improves code readability and makes it easier for others to understand your work.
- Abstraction: Hide complex implementation details behind clear and concise interfaces. This allows developers to use modules without needing to know their internal workings.

Version Control:

Use version control systems like **Git** to track changes, collaborate with team members, and easily roll back to previous versions if needed.

Developers use version control to:

- Track Changes: Version control allows developers to monitor changes made to files over time. Each modification is documented, providing a detailed history of who made the changes and when.
- Collaborate Effectively: Multiple developers can work on the same project simultaneously without interfering with each other's code. Version control facilitates collaboration by merging changes made by different team members.
- Branching and Merging: Developers can create branches to work on specific features or bug fixes independently. Once the changes are complete, branches can be merged back into the main codebase, preventing conflicts and ensuring a smooth integration of new features.
- Revert to Previous Versions: In case of errors or unforeseen issues, developers can easily revert to a previous version of the code. This helps maintain code stability and quickly address problems that may arise.
- Backup and Restore: Version control serves as a backup mechanism, safeguarding against data loss. Developers can restore previous versions of the project if the need arises, providing an added layer of security.
- Facilitate Code Reviews: Version control systems support code review processes by allowing team members to review proposed changes before they are merged into the main codebase. This promotes code quality and helps catch potential issues early on.

Overall, version control is an indispensable tool for web development teams, promoting collaboration, code quality, and project stability throughout the development lifecycle.

Accessibility (WCAG Guidelines):

Design and develop with accessibility in mind, adhering to Web Content Accessibility Guidelines (WCAG) to ensure your website is usable by people with disabilities.

Accessibility in web development refers to the practice of designing and developing websites and web applications in a way that ensures equal access and usability for people with diverse abilities and disabilities. The Web Content Accessibility Guidelines (WCAG) are a set of internationally recognized standards developed by the World Wide Web Consortium (W3C) to help guide web developers in creating more accessible digital content. Here are key aspects of WCAG guidelines:

Perceivable:
- Text Alternatives: Provide text descriptions (alt text) for non-text content like images, graphs, and charts to ensure that screen readers can convey the information to users with visual impairments.
- Captions and Transcripts: Include captions for multimedia content and provide transcripts for audio content to assist users with hearing impairments.

Operable:

- Keyboard Accessibility: Ensure that all functionality is accessible using a keyboard. This is crucial for users who cannot use a mouse or other pointing devices.
- Navigable and Intuitive: Design navigation and interactive elements in a predictable and consistent manner, allowing users to understand and operate them easily.

Understandable:
- Readable Text: Use clear and legible text with adjustable font sizes. Provide sufficient contrast between text and background to enhance readability.
- Consistent Navigation: Maintain consistency in navigation and page layout to help users understand the structure of the content.

Robust:
- Compatibility: Ensure compatibility with current and future technologies, including assistive technologies. Code should be valid, well-structured, and capable of adapting to evolving standards.

Implementing WCAG guidelines not only ensures legal compliance in many jurisdictions but also contributes to a more inclusive digital environment. By making websites and web applications accessible, developers can reach a broader audience and create a more user-friendly experience for everyone, regardless of their abilities or disabilities.

Progressive Enhancement:

Implement a progressive enhancement strategy, starting with a baseline experience and progressively adding advanced features for users with modern browsers or devices.

Progressive Enhancement is a web development approach that focuses on delivering a basic, functional experience to all users, regardless of their device or browser capabilities, and then progressively enhancing that experience for users with more advanced technology. The core principle is to start with a solid foundation and add enhancements based on the capabilities of the user's device and browser. This approach ensures a broader reach and a more inclusive user experience. Here are key aspects of Progressive Enhancement:

Basic HTML Structure:
- Semantics: Begin with well-structured, semantic HTML to provide a meaningful foundation for all users. Semantic markup helps ensure content is properly understood by a variety of devices, including assistive technologies.

CSS for Styling:
- Responsive Design: Use CSS to create a responsive layout that adapts to different screen sizes. This ensures that the content is accessible and

readable on a variety of devices, from large desktop monitors to small mobile screens.
- Graceful Degradation: Apply CSS styles for aesthetics and layout but ensure that the absence of certain styles doesn't break the core functionality of the website. This allows the site to gracefully degrade on browsers or devices that don't support advanced styling.

JavaScript for Enhancement:
- Progressive Enhancement with JavaScript: Introduce JavaScript to enhance the user experience progressively. For example, use JavaScript to add interactive features, validate forms, or load additional content dynamically.
- Feature Detection: Employ feature detection rather than browser detection to identify the capabilities of the user's device. This allows developers to adapt the experience based on what the browser can support.

Accessibility Considerations:
- Keyboard Navigation: Ensure that the website is navigable and usable via keyboard input. This is especially important for users with disabilities who rely on keyboard navigation or assistive technologies.
- Alt Text for Images: Provide descriptive alternative text for images to make content accessible to users with visual impairments.

Performance Optimization:
- Optimize Assets: Optimize images, scripts, and stylesheets to minimize page load times. Faster loading pages benefit users on slower network connections and less powerful devices.

Testing Across Browsers and Devices:
- Cross-Browser Compatibility: Test the website across different browsers to ensure a consistent and functional experience for users regardless of their browser choice.
- Device Testing: Test on various devices to ensure compatibility and functionality across a range of screen sizes and resolutions.

Progressive Enhancement aligns with the principle of inclusive design, making web content accessible to a wide range of users with different devices, network conditions, and abilities. By starting with a core experience and building upon it, developers can create a more robust and user-friendly web experience for everyone.

Regular Backups:

Regularly back up your website and its data to prevent data loss in case of unforeseen events or security breaches.

Regular backups are a fundamental aspect of web development that involves creating and storing copies of a website's data, files, and configurations at specific points in time. This practice is essential for mitigating the risk of data loss and ensuring the ability to restore a website to a previous state in the event of unforeseen issues, such as hardware failures, software errors, or security breaches. Here are key aspects of regular backups in web development:

Data Protection:
- Content Preservation: Regular backups safeguard the website's content, including text, images, databases, and any other critical data. This is crucial for preserving the integrity of the website's information.

Security Measures:
- Protection Against Cyber Threats: Backups serve as a safety net in case of security incidents, such as hacking or malware attacks. If a website is compromised, having recent backups allows developers to restore a clean version of the site.

Disaster Recovery:
- Mitigating Data Loss: In the event of hardware failures, server crashes, or accidental deletions, regular backups ensure that a website can be restored to a previous state. This minimizes downtime and prevents significant data loss.

Website Updates and Changes:
- Before Updates: Before making significant updates to a website, such as applying software updates or implementing new features, it's advisable to perform a backup. This provides a fallback option in case the updates cause unexpected issues.

Backup Frequency:
- Regular Schedule: Establish a consistent schedule for backups, whether it's daily, weekly, or in accordance with the website's update frequency. The backup frequency should align with the frequency of changes to the website's content and configurations.

Offsite Storage:
- Cloud or External Servers: Store backups in locations separate from the primary server. This could include cloud storage services or external servers. Offsite backups protect against data loss in case the primary server experiences a catastrophic failure.

Automation:
- Automated Backup Systems: Implement automated backup systems to streamline the process and ensure backups are consistently performed at scheduled intervals. Automation reduces the risk of human error and ensures the reliability of the backup process.

Testing Backups:
- Verification of Integrity: Regularly test backups to ensure their integrity and viability for restoration. It's important to know that the backup process is functioning correctly and that the data can be successfully restored when needed.

Documentation:

- Record Keeping: Maintain documentation of the backup process, including the schedule, storage locations, and procedures for restoration. Clear documentation helps streamline recovery efforts in case of emergencies.

Regular backups are a proactive measure that can save time, resources, and data integrity in the long run. By incorporating regular backup practices into web development workflows, developers and website administrators can enhance the overall resilience of a website and minimize the impact of unforeseen events.

Optimized Images:

Compress and optimize images to reduce file sizes without compromising quality, improving page load times.

Optimizing images is a critical aspect of web development that involves reducing the file size of images while maintaining acceptable visual quality. This process is essential for improving website performance, reducing loading times, and enhancing the overall user experience. Here are key considerations and techniques for optimized images in web development:

File Formats:
- Choose the Right Format: Select the appropriate image file format based on the content. For photographs and images with many colors, JPEG is often suitable, while PNG is preferred for images with transparency or sharp edges. WebP is an emerging format that offers a good balance between compression and quality.

Compression:
- Lossless vs. Lossy Compression: Use compression techniques to reduce file size. Lossless compression retains the original image quality but may not achieve as much reduction in file size as lossy compression, which sacrifices some quality for smaller file sizes. The choice depends on the specific use case.

Image Dimensions:
- Resize Images: Scale images to their display size on the web. Uploading excessively large images and relying on HTML or CSS to resize them can lead to unnecessary data transfer and slower loading times.

Responsive Images:
- Implement Responsive Images: Use the srcset attribute to provide multiple versions of an image based on different screen sizes and resolutions. This ensures that users receive appropriately sized images, reducing unnecessary data transfer for smaller screens.

Lazy Loading:
- Lazy Loading: Implement lazy loading to defer the loading of images until they are about to enter the user's viewport. This technique helps prioritize the loading of visible content, improving initial page load times.

Image Sprites:

- Sprite Sheets: Combine small images, icons, or buttons into sprite sheets. This reduces the number of server requests and minimizes the loading time by delivering multiple images in a single request.

Image Compression Tools:
- Online Tools and Software: Utilize various image compression tools and software to automatically compress images without compromising quality. Popular tools include ImageOptim, TinyPNG, and JPEGoptim.

Image Delivery Networks (CDNs):
- CDN Integration: Integrate with Content Delivery Networks (CDNs) that automatically optimize and deliver images from servers located strategically around the world. This reduces latency and accelerates image loading times.

WebP Format and Modern Image Formats:
- Adopt Modern Formats: Explore newer image formats such as WebP, which offers superior compression and quality compared to traditional formats like JPEG and PNG. Ensure browser compatibility or provide fallbacks for unsupported browsers.

Image Accessibility:
- Alt Text: Include descriptive alternative text (alt text) for images to ensure accessibility for users with visual impairments. Alt text also contributes to search engine optimization (SEO).

Optimizing images is a continuous process that involves finding the right balance between file size and visual quality. By implementing these practices, web developers can significantly enhance website performance, reduce bandwidth usage, and provide a more efficient and enjoyable experience for users.

Content Delivery Network (CDN):

Utilize CDNs to distribute website content across multiple servers globally, reducing latency and improving loading speeds for users worldwide.

A Content Delivery Network (CDN) is a distributed network of servers strategically located around the world to deliver web content, such as images, stylesheets, scripts, and other static assets, to users more efficiently. CDNs enhance the performance, reliability, and scalability of websites by reducing latency, minimizing server load, and optimizing content delivery. Here are key aspects of Content Delivery Networks for websites:

Global Content Distribution:
- Server Locations: CDNs operate servers in various geographical locations, known as points of presence (PoPs). This global distribution ensures that content is physically closer to users, reducing the time it takes to fetch and load web resources.

Faster Loading Times:

- Reduced Latency: By serving content from servers geographically closer to the user, CDNs minimize latency and accelerate the loading times of web pages. This is particularly beneficial for users accessing websites from different regions.

Load Balancing:
- Distributed Load: CDNs distribute the load across multiple servers, preventing a single server from becoming a bottleneck. This load balancing enhances website performance and ensures a consistent experience for users, even during traffic spikes.

Caching Mechanisms:
- Content Caching: CDNs employ caching mechanisms to store static content temporarily on servers. This reduces the need to fetch resources from the origin server every time a user requests them, leading to faster response times.

Security Improvements:
- Distributed Security: CDNs provide an additional layer of security by absorbing and mitigating Distributed Denial of Service (DDoS) attacks. The distributed nature of the network helps handle large-scale attacks more effectively.

Scalability:
- Elasticity: CDNs offer scalability to accommodate varying levels of website traffic. As the demand for content increases, CDNs can dynamically scale resources to ensure optimal performance without overburdening the origin server.

HTTPS Support:
- SSL/TLS Acceleration: CDNs often include built-in support for SSL/TLS encryption, accelerating secure connections and reducing the computational burden on the origin server.

Streaming and Dynamic Content:
- Media Delivery: CDNs can handle the delivery of streaming media, such as videos and live broadcasts, optimizing the user experience for multimedia content.
- Dynamic Content Acceleration: Some CDNs are designed to accelerate the delivery of dynamically generated content, improving the performance of web applications and personalized experiences.

Cost Efficiency:
- Bandwidth Savings: CDNs can result in cost savings by reducing the amount of data transferred from the origin server. This is particularly beneficial for websites with heavy traffic and large media files.

Analytics and Monitoring:
- Performance Analytics: CDNs often provide analytics tools that offer insights into website performance, user behavior, and traffic patterns. This information can be valuable for optimizing content delivery strategies.

Implementing a CDN is a best practice for websites seeking to enhance speed, reliability, and global accessibility. By leveraging the capabilities of CDNs, web developers can significantly improve the overall user experience and ensure the efficient delivery of content to a diverse audience.

Here are some popular CDNs:

Cloudflare:
- Free Plan: Cloudflare offers a free plan with features such as CDN, DDoS protection, SSL/TLS encryption, and basic performance optimization. It has a large global network and is known for its user-friendly interface.

Akamai:
- Enterprise and Free Trials: Akamai is a leading enterprise-grade CDN, but it also provides free trials for testing its services. It offers a wide range of features, including content delivery, security, and performance optimization.

Fastly:
- Free Trial: Fastly is a high-performance CDN that provides a free trial. It emphasizes real-time content delivery and offers features like instant purging, dynamic content acceleration, and edge computing capabilities.

Netlify:
- Free Plan: Netlify offers a free plan that includes CDN services, continuous deployment, and serverless functions. It is particularly popular among developers for hosting static sites and deploying modern web applications.

GitHub Pages:
- Free for Public Repositories: GitHub Pages is a CDN service provided by GitHub. It's free for hosting static websites directly from a GitHub repository. While it's more suitable for static content, it's a straightforward and cost-effective option for hosting.

jsDelivr:
- Open Source CDN: jsDelivr is an open-source CDN that allows developers to load JavaScript libraries, jQuery plugins, fonts, and other assets directly from a CDN. It's easy to integrate and doesn't require registration.

Cloudinary:
- Free Tier: Cloudinary is primarily known for image and video management but also provides CDN services. It has a free tier with limited resources and is popular for optimizing and delivering media assets.

KeyCDN:
- Pay-as-you-go: While KeyCDN is a paid CDN, it operates on a pay-as-you-go model, making it accessible for smaller websites. It provides features such as HTTP/2, free SSL, and real-time analytics.

BunnyCDN:
- Affordable Plans: BunnyCDN is known for its cost-effective plans and global coverage. It offers features like instant purging, HTTP/2 support, and real-time analytics. The pay-as-you-go model makes it suitable for various budgets.

Swarmify:
- Free Tier: Swarmify offers a free plan with limited bandwidth. It specializes in video delivery and provides features like adaptive streaming and intelligent video acceleration.

When selecting a CDN, it's essential to consider factors such as the specific needs of your website, the geographical distribution of your audience, available features, ease of integration, and any associated costs beyond free plans. Many CDNs offer a range of services, from basic content delivery to advanced security features, allowing you to choose a solution that best aligns with your requirements.

Testing Environment:

Develop and test in a dedicated environment to catch and fix issues before deploying changes to the live site.

A testing environment in web development is a dedicated setup where developers can test and validate their code, applications, and websites before deploying them to a live or production environment. A well-structured testing environment helps identify and address issues, ensures the reliability of the code, and provides a controlled space for quality assurance. Here are key components and considerations for a testing environment in web development:

Development and Staging Environments:
- Development Environment: Developers initially work in a local development environment on their own machines. This allows them to experiment, code, and debug without affecting shared resources.
- Staging Environment: Staging is a more controlled environment that closely resembles the production environment. It serves as an intermediate step between development and production for final testing and validation.

Server and Database Replication:
- Environment Mirroring: The testing environment should mirror the production environment as closely as possible. This includes replicating server configurations, databases, and other relevant settings to ensure consistency.

Version Control:
- Code Repository: Utilize version control systems (e.g., Git) to manage and track changes to the codebase. This ensures that developers can collaborate seamlessly, and code changes are easily traceable.

Automated Testing:
- Test Automation Tools: Implement automated testing tools for unit testing, integration testing, and end-to-end testing. Automated tests help catch regressions and ensure that code changes do not introduce new issues.

Continuous Integration (CI):

- CI Pipeline: Integrate a CI system (e.g., Jenkins, Travis CI) to automate the process of building, testing, and validating code changes. CI ensures that new code is continuously integrated and tested as developers make changes.

Isolation of Environments:
- Isolation: Keep testing environments isolated from the production environment to prevent unintended consequences. Use separate databases, servers, and configurations to avoid conflicts.

Performance Testing:
- Load Testing: Conduct performance testing to assess how the application performs under different load conditions. Tools like JMeter or Gatling can simulate various user interactions and assess system scalability.

Security Testing:
- Vulnerability Scanning: Perform regular security testing, including vulnerability scanning and penetration testing, to identify and address potential security risks.

Environment Configuration Management:
- Configuration Files: Manage environment configurations through configuration files. This helps ensure consistency and makes it easier to replicate the environment when needed.

User Acceptance Testing (UAT):
- UAT Environment: Create a separate environment specifically for user acceptance testing. This allows stakeholders, including non-technical users, to validate that the application meets business requirements before deployment.

Logging and Monitoring:
- Log Analysis: Implement logging mechanisms to capture relevant information during testing. Monitor the system for errors, performance issues, and other anomalies to identify and address issues proactively.

Backup and Recovery Procedures:
- Backup Protocols: Establish backup and recovery procedures for testing environments. This ensures that in the event of data loss or configuration issues, developers can quickly restore the environment to a known state.

Having a well-structured testing environment is integral to the software development lifecycle. It promotes collaboration among team members, ensures code quality, and reduces the likelihood of issues reaching the production environment. Regular testing and validation in a controlled environment contribute to the overall stability and reliability of web applications.

User-Centric Design:

Prioritize user experience with intuitive navigation, clear calls to action, and user-friendly interfaces.

User-Centric Design is an approach that places the needs and experiences of users at the forefront of the design process. It involves understanding user behaviors, preferences, and pain points through research and feedback, then using this insight to inform the design and development of products or services. The goal is to create intuitive, enjoyable, and effective solutions that resonate with users, ultimately leading to higher satisfaction and usability. This iterative process often involves usability testing, prototyping, and continuous refinement based on user input, ensuring that the final product aligns closely with user expectations and needs.

Regular Code Reviews:

Conduct regular code reviews within your development team to identify potential issues, ensure coding standards are followed, and share knowledge.

Regular code reviews are a fundamental practice in web development that involves systematically examining and assessing the code written by team members. This collaborative process contributes to code quality, identifies potential issues early on, and fosters knowledge sharing within the development team. Here are key aspects of regular code reviews in web development:

Quality Assurance:
- Bug Detection: Code reviews help identify and catch bugs, errors, or potential security vulnerabilities before the code is merged into the main codebase.
- Coding Standards: Reviews ensure that the code adheres to established coding standards, promoting consistency and readability across the entire project.

Knowledge Sharing:
- Collaboration: Code reviews provide an opportunity for team members to collaborate and share knowledge. Junior developers can learn from more experienced team members, fostering a culture of continuous learning and improvement.
- Code Ownership: Shared understanding of the codebase is enhanced, reducing the risk of knowledge silos. Multiple team members become familiar with different parts of the code.

Code Consistency:
- Coding Guidelines: Enforcing coding guidelines and best practices through code reviews helps maintain a consistent coding style throughout the project. This consistency improves readability and makes the codebase more maintainable.

Early Detection of Issues:
- Preventing Future Problems: Detecting and addressing issues early in the development process helps prevent the accumulation of technical debt and reduces the likelihood of more significant problems later on.

Learning Opportunities:

- Mentoring: Code reviews offer a mentoring opportunity for team members. Senior developers can provide constructive feedback, share insights, and help junior developers improve their coding skills.
- Continuous Improvement: Regular reviews create a feedback loop for developers to learn from each other and continuously improve their coding practices.

Code Performance:
- Optimization: Code reviews may highlight opportunities for code optimization and performance improvements. This ensures that the application runs efficiently and meets performance expectations.

Code Documentation:
- Documentation Checks: Code reviews include a check for the quality and completeness of code documentation. Well-documented code is essential for understanding functionality, especially when different team members work on the same project.

Tool Integration:
- Automated Tools: Integrate automated code analysis tools into the code review process to catch issues related to code style, security, and potential bugs. This helps streamline the review process and ensures consistency.

Code Review Etiquette:
- Constructive Feedback: Encourage a culture of providing constructive feedback during code reviews. Focus on improvements rather than criticism and create an environment where team members feel comfortable sharing and receiving feedback.

Regular Schedule:
- Consistent Reviews: Establish a regular schedule for code reviews to maintain a steady and predictable flow. This consistency ensures that code is thoroughly reviewed without causing bottlenecks in the development process.

Regular code reviews play a crucial role in maintaining a high standard of code quality, fostering collaboration, and creating a culture of continuous improvement within web development teams.

Graceful Degradation:

Plan for graceful degradation by ensuring your website functions reasonably well even if certain features are not supported in older browsers.

Content Management System (CMS) Best Practices:

If using a CMS, follow best practices for secure configuration, regularly update plugins/themes, and customize settings to align with your website's goals.

Content Management Systems (CMS) are crucial tools for creating, managing, and organizing digital content on websites. To ensure optimal performance, security, and user experience, consider the following best practices when working with CMS:

Choose the Right CMS:
- Select a CMS that aligns with your specific needs, scalability requirements, and technical expertise. Popular CMS options include WordPress, Joomla, Drupal, and others, each with its strengths and weaknesses.

Keep Software Updated:
- Regularly update the CMS core, themes, and plugins/modules to patch security vulnerabilities, improve performance, and access new features. Staying up-to-date is essential for maintaining a secure and efficient website.

Use Secure Authentication:
- Implement strong authentication mechanisms, such as two-factor authentication (2FA), to enhance the security of the CMS login process and protect against unauthorized access.

Secure User Roles and Permissions:
- Assign roles and permissions carefully to restrict user access based on responsibilities. Limit administrative privileges to only those who require them to reduce the risk of misuse.

Backup Regularly:
- Set up regular backups of your CMS and website data. This ensures a quick recovery in case of data loss, accidental changes, or security incidents. Test backup restoration procedures periodically.

Optimize Images and Media:
- Compress and optimize images and media files before uploading them to the CMS. This improves page load times and contributes to a better user experience.

SEO-Friendly URLs:
- Configure clean, descriptive, and SEO-friendly URLs for your content. This not only enhances search engine optimization but also improves the usability of your website.

Implement Caching:
- Utilize caching mechanisms to reduce server load and speed up page load times. This is especially important for dynamic websites that generate content on the fly.

Responsive Design:
- Ensure that your chosen CMS and website theme support responsive design, providing a consistent and user-friendly experience across various devices and screen sizes.

Monitor Website Performance:
- Use monitoring tools to track website performance, identify bottlenecks, and address issues promptly. This includes monitoring server resource usage, page load times, and overall site availability.

Content Governance:
- Establish content governance policies to maintain consistency, quality, and relevance of content. Clearly define roles and responsibilities for content creation, review, and publication.

Security Audits and Scans:
- Conduct regular security audits and vulnerability scans to identify and address potential security threats. Address any vulnerabilities promptly to protect against cyberattacks.

User Training:
- Provide training for content editors and administrators to ensure they understand how to use the CMS efficiently and follow best practices for content creation and management.

Accessibility Considerations:
- Design and structure your content with accessibility in mind. Ensure that your website is usable by people with disabilities, following Web Content Accessibility Guidelines (WCAG) standards.

Community Support and Documentation:
- Choose a CMS with a strong community and well-documented resources. This ensures that you have access to support, tutorials, and updates to stay informed and troubleshoot issues effectively.

By following these best practices, you can maximize the effectiveness of your Content Management System, create a more secure and efficient website, and provide a positive experience for both content creators and end-users.

Monitor and Analyze Performance:

Use tools like Google Analytics to monitor website performance, track user behavior, and gather insights for continuous improvement.

Continuous Learning:

Stay updated on the latest web development trends, technologies, and best practices to ensure your skills remain relevant in this rapidly evolving field.

Earn from freelancing

Embarking on a freelance web development career is an exciting venture that allows you to leverage your coding prowess to build a thriving business. In this practical guide, we'll explore actionable steps to kickstart your freelancing journey and secure meaningful projects.

1. Craft an Impressive Portfolio:

Begin by creating a visually appealing and comprehensive portfolio that showcases your best work. Include diverse projects that highlight your proficiency in web development, from responsive design to e-commerce solutions.

2. Define Your Niche:

Consider specializing in a specific niche, such as WordPress development or mobile app design. Specialization not only sets you apart in the market but also attracts clients seeking expertise in their particular industry.

3. Establish a Professional Online Presence:

Create a professional website showcasing your portfolio, skills, and client testimonials. Simultaneously, optimize your LinkedIn profile to enhance your visibility within the professional community.

4. Join Freelance Platforms:

Register on popular freelance platforms like Upwork, Freelancer, or Fiverr. Develop a compelling profile that clearly outlines your skills, experience, and the value you bring to clients. Actively bid on projects aligned with your expertise.

5. Network Actively:

Attend both local and virtual networking events to connect with potential clients and fellow freelancers. Engage in industry forums and social media groups to expand your network and discover new opportunities.

6. Clearly Define Your Services:

Articulate the web development services you offer, emphasizing your strengths and capabilities. This clarity helps clients understand your expertise and align their needs with your skills.

7. Set Competitive Pricing:

Research market rates to establish competitive pricing for your services. Consider the complexity of projects, your level of expertise, and the value you provide when determining your rates.

8. Upskill Continuously:

Stay abreast of the latest web development trends and technologies. Regularly upskill to remain competitive, and consider acquiring certifications that enhance your credibility within the freelance market.

9. Provide Outstanding Customer Service:

Prioritize effective communication, set clear expectations, and keep clients informed throughout the project lifecycle. A positive client experience leads to client satisfaction, repeat business, and valuable referrals.

10. Offer Post-Development Services:

Consider providing maintenance and support packages to clients. Offering ongoing support after the project completion not only ensures client satisfaction but also positions you as a reliable long-term partner.

Embarking on a freelancing career in web development requires a combination of skill, strategy, and a proactive mindset. By crafting a compelling portfolio, specializing in a niche, networking actively, and delivering exceptional customer service, you can lay a solid foundation for a successful freelancing journey. Stay adaptable, continuously enhance your skills, and watch as your freelance web development business thrives in the dynamic digital landscape.

Earn from your Websites

For aspiring web developers, the journey goes beyond crafting compelling code—it extends into transforming your skills into a lucrative venture. One powerful avenue is leveraging your website to generate income. In this guide, we'll explore diverse strategies for monetizing your website and turning your passion for web development into a sustainable income stream.

1. Establish Your Online Presence:

Before diving into monetization strategies, ensure your website serves as a strong foundation. Design a clean, user-friendly interface, optimize for mobile responsiveness, and create engaging, high-quality content. A professional and well-maintained website is your canvas for future monetization endeavors.

2. Explore Ad Revenue:

Ad revenue is a classic method of monetization. Platforms like Google AdSense allow you to display ads on your website, earning revenue when visitors click or view these ads. However, striking a balance is crucial—too many ads can deter users, impacting your website's overall experience.

3. Affiliate Marketing:

Joining affiliate programs lets you earn a commission by promoting products or services. Incorporate affiliate links naturally within your content, recommending products relevant to your audience. Be transparent about your affiliations to build trust with your visitors.

4. Sell Digital Products:

Leverage your expertise to create and sell digital products. Whether it's coding tutorials, e-books, or design templates, your audience may be eager to purchase educational or time-saving resources directly from your website. Platforms like Gumroad and Sellfy simplify the selling process.

5. Offer Online Courses:

Consider sharing your web development skills through online courses. Platforms like Udemy and Teachable allow you to create and sell courses, providing value to your audience while generating income.

6. Freelance Services:

Promote your web development skills by offering freelance services directly through your website. Create a portfolio showcasing your work, set clear service offerings, and incorporate a user-friendly contact form for potential clients.

7. Subscription Models:

Introduce subscription-based models for premium content or services. Whether it's a members-only section with exclusive resources or a subscription-based newsletter, recurring revenue can contribute to the financial sustainability of your website.

8. Host Webinars or Virtual Events:

Engage with your audience through webinars or virtual events. Monetize these experiences through ticket sales, sponsorships, or partnerships with relevant brands. This not only generates income but also enhances your authority within the web development community.

9. Donations and Crowdfunding:

Enable donation options on your website for visitors who appreciate your content. Platforms like Patreon or Buy Me a Coffee provide easy ways for your audience to support you financially.

Monetizing your website as a web developer is a journey that requires creativity, dedication, and a deep understanding of your audience. By combining your technical skills with smart business strategies, you can turn your website into a valuable asset that not only showcases your expertise but also generates a sustainable income. Remember, the key is to deliver value to your audience while finding monetization methods that align with your brand and resonate with your visitors. As you embark on this exciting endeavor, let the synergy between your passion for web development and your entrepreneurial spirit drive your success.

Earn from selling Web Applications

For passionate web developers, the thrill of code isn't confined to just building functional applications. The entrepreneurial spirit whispers another exciting prospect: selling your creations. Stepping into the world of web application sales opens doors to financial independence, creative freedom, and the chance to directly impact users' lives. But where do you start? Let's explore the opportunities brimming in this realm:

1. Craft Solutions, Solve Problems:

Think beyond basic websites. Identify real-world problems and craft web applications that offer elegant solutions. Imagine building a platform that connects pet sitters with busy owners, or an app that streamlines grocery shopping for families. The possibilities are endless. By focusing on genuine needs, you'll attract a dedicated user base and secure a competitive edge.

2. Choose Your Monetization Model:

Selling web applications isn't a one-size-fits-all game. You have diverse options:

- Subscriptions: Offer recurring access to your app's features, building a steady income stream. Think SaaS models like Spotify or Canva.
- One-time purchases: Sell licenses for permanent access to your app, ideal for niche solutions with fixed functionalities.
- Freemium model: Allow free basic features with premium upgrades for advanced functionality, catering to both budget-conscious and power users.
- In-app purchases: Offer additional features or content within the app for users who want to enhance their experience.

3. Marketing is Your Magic Wand:

Building a great app is only half the battle. You need to reach your target audience. Master the art of marketing:

- Content marketing: Create blog posts, tutorials, and videos showcasing your app's benefits.
- Social media engagement: Connect with potential users on platforms like Twitter and LinkedIn.

- Leverage user reviews: Encourage satisfied users to leave positive reviews and testimonials.

4. Embrace the Community:

Don't go it alone. Web development is a vibrant community with forums, conferences, and online groups. Seek support, share experiences, and learn from seasoned entrepreneurs. Collaboration can spark new ideas and open doors to valuable partnerships.

5. The Journey is the Reward:

Building and selling web applications is not a get-rich-quick scheme. It's a marathon, not a sprint. Be prepared for challenges, adapt to market trends, and constantly refine your product. The satisfaction of seeing your creation solve real-world problems is a reward in itself.

Remember, web application entrepreneurship is an exciting path for aspiring developers. With the right mix of creativity, technical prowess, and marketing savvy, you can turn your code into a thriving business. So, embrace the challenge, unleash your inner entrepreneur, and build your dream web application empire!

I earned significant money from our Timesheet application. Apart from earning money by selling the source code of the application, I could earn further by doing freelance work for the app buyers.

Web Hosting Providers

Hosting providers play a crucial role in making websites accessible on the internet. They offer services that allow individuals and businesses to store and manage their website files, databases, and other resources on servers connected to the internet. Here's an overview of hosting providers and key considerations when choosing one:

Types of Hosting:

Shared Hosting:
- *Description:* Multiple websites share resources on a single server.
- *Pros:* Cost-effective, easy to manage for beginners.
- *Cons:* Limited resources, potential performance impact if other sites on the server experience high traffic.

VPS Hosting (Virtual Private Server):
- *Description:* Virtual partitioning of a physical server, providing dedicated resources to each virtual server.

- *Pros:* More control and resources than shared hosting, scalable.
- *Cons:* Requires more technical knowledge than shared hosting.

Dedicated Hosting:
- *Description:* Entire server dedicated to a single user or entity.
- *Pros:* Maximum control and customization, high performance.
- *Cons:* Higher cost, requires server management skills or a managed hosting service.

Cloud Hosting:
- *Description:* Resources are distributed across multiple servers, offering scalability and redundancy.
- *Pros:* High availability, scalability, pay-as-you-go pricing.
- *Cons:* Costs can scale with usage, and some technical expertise is required.

Managed WordPress Hosting:
- *Description:* Hosting optimized specifically for WordPress websites.
- *Pros:* WordPress-specific optimizations, automatic updates, and security features.
- *Cons:* Usually more expensive than shared hosting.

Key Considerations When Choosing a Hosting Provider:

Performance:
- Check for server reliability, uptime guarantees, and server response times.

Scalability:
- Consider future growth and ensure the hosting provider can accommodate increased traffic and resource needs.

Security:
- Look for security features such as firewalls, SSL certificates, and regular backups.

Support:
- Evaluate the level of customer support offered—24/7 support, live chat, ticket system, etc.

Ease of Use:
- Consider the user interface and ease of managing your hosting account and website.

Cost:
- Understand the pricing structure, including any hidden fees. Consider your budget and the value provided.

Server Location:
- Choose a server location that aligns with your target audience to ensure faster load times.

Features:
- Check for features like one-click installations, email hosting, content delivery network (CDN) integration, and more.

Reviews and Reputation:
- Research customer reviews and the reputation of the hosting provider.

Backup and Restore Options:

- Ensure that the hosting provider offers regular backups and easy restoration options.

Popular Hosting Providers:

Bluehost:
- Known for WordPress hosting, shared hosting, and ease of use.

SiteGround:
- Offers shared, cloud, and dedicated hosting with excellent customer support.

HostGator:
- Provides a range of hosting solutions with a user-friendly interface.

AWS (Amazon Web Services):
- A cloud hosting platform with a wide array of services for scalable and customizable hosting.

DigitalOcean:
- Specializes in cloud infrastructure with a developer-friendly platform.

GoDaddy:
- Offers a variety of hosting services, domain registration, and website-building tools.

Choosing the right hosting provider depends on your specific needs, budget, and technical requirements. It's essential to assess your goals and match them with a provider that aligns with your web hosting needs.

Leveraging WordPress for Earning Money

WordPress, originally a robust blogging platform, has evolved into a versatile content management system (CMS) that powers over 40% of the web. Beyond its user-friendly interface and customization capabilities, WordPress offers abundant opportunities for aspiring entrepreneurs and web developers to turn their passion into profit. In this article, we'll explore the myriad ways you can leverage WordPress to earn money.

1. Building and Selling WordPress Themes:

One lucrative avenue is designing and selling WordPress themes. With the ever-growing demand for visually appealing and functional websites, a well-crafted theme can find a market. Platforms like ThemeForest allow you to showcase and sell your themes to a global audience.

2. Developing Custom WordPress Plugins:

Extend WordPress functionality by creating custom plugins. Whether it's enhancing SEO, improving security, or introducing unique features, there's a vast market for plugins. Consider offering free versions with premium upgrades for added revenue.

3. Freelance WordPress Development:

Tap into the vast world of freelancing by offering your WordPress development services. Platforms like Upwork and Fiverr connect you with clients seeking WordPress expertise. Build a portfolio, highlight your skills, and bid competitively to secure projects.

4. Starting a WordPress Blog:

Blogging remains a powerful way to generate income. Use WordPress to share your insights, expertise, or niche-focused content. Monetize through ads, affiliate marketing, sponsored posts, or by offering premium content to a loyal subscriber base.

5. Creating and Selling Online Courses:

Leverage your WordPress website to host and sell online courses. Plugins like LearnDash and Teachable seamlessly integrate with WordPress, allowing you to share your knowledge while generating revenue.

6. Affiliate Marketing Through WordPress:

Integrate affiliate marketing into your WordPress strategy. Promote products or services related to your niche through affiliate links. As your audience trusts your recommendations, you can earn commissions for each sale generated through your unique links.

7. Offering Membership Programs:

Transform your WordPress site into an exclusive community by offering membership programs. Provide premium content, special access, or personalized services in exchange for a subscription fee, creating a recurring revenue stream.

8. E-commerce with WooCommerce:

WooCommerce, a WordPress plugin, turns your site into a fully functional online store. Sell physical or digital products, manage inventory, and implement various payment gateways. E-commerce offers diverse revenue streams for entrepreneurs.

9. Providing WordPress Consultation Services:

Offer your expertise through WordPress consultation services. Help businesses optimize their WordPress websites, troubleshoot issues, or plan for future developments. Charge hourly or on a project basis.

10. Host Webinars and Workshops:

Engage your audience by hosting webinars and workshops on your WordPress site. Charge a fee for access, and use these events to share valuable insights, demonstrate your expertise, and connect with your community.

WordPress isn't just a platform for creating websites; it's a gateway to a myriad of income-generating opportunities. By combining your passion for web development with strategic business ventures, you can unlock the full potential of WordPress. Whether you're crafting themes, developing plugins, or building an online empire through blogging and e-commerce, WordPress provides the tools and flexibility needed to turn your digital presence into a thriving source of income. Embrace the versatility of WordPress, stay innovative, and let your entrepreneurial spirit flourish in the dynamic world of online business.

Leveraging AI for Revolutionary Web Development

As technology advances, artificial intelligence (AI) has emerged as a transformative force, reshaping industries across the globe. In the realm of web development, AI is not just a buzzword but a catalyst for innovation, efficiency, and enhanced user experiences. This article explores how harnessing the power of AI can propel web development into a new era.

1. Automated Code Generation:

AI-powered tools are revolutionizing the way code is written. Developers can now utilize code generators that leverage machine learning algorithms to understand project requirements and automatically produce high-quality code. This accelerates development timelines and reduces the likelihood of errors, enabling teams to focus on more strategic aspects of the project.

2. Intelligent Design Assistance:

AI is becoming a design ally, assisting developers in creating visually appealing and user-friendly interfaces. Design tools powered by AI can analyze design trends, user behavior, and industry standards to suggest layout optimizations, color schemes, and interactive elements, streamlining the design process and ensuring a modern and engaging user experience.

3. Predictive Analytics for User Behavior:

Understanding user behavior is critical for effective web development. AI-driven analytics tools can analyze vast amounts of data to predict user preferences, navigation patterns, and potential bottlenecks. Armed with these insights, developers can tailor websites to meet user expectations, leading to improved engagement and conversion rates.

4. Personalized User Experiences:

AI enables the creation of highly personalized web experiences. By analyzing user data in real-time, AI algorithms can dynamically adjust content, recommendations, and interfaces to match individual preferences. This level of personalization enhances user satisfaction and contributes to increased user retention and loyalty.

5. Chatbots and Virtual Assistants:

Incorporating AI-driven chatbots and virtual assistants enhances user interactions. These intelligent systems can provide real-time support, answer queries, and guide users through website functionalities. By automating routine tasks, they free up human resources for more complex problem-solving and creative aspects of web development.

6. Natural Language Processing (NLP):

NLP capabilities in AI facilitate seamless interactions between users and websites. Chat interfaces, search functionalities, and content creation can benefit from NLP, enabling websites to better understand and respond to user input, resulting in a more intuitive and user-friendly experience.

7. Automated Testing and Bug Detection:

AI streamlines the testing process by automating test case generation and execution. AI-powered testing tools can identify potential bugs, vulnerabilities, and performance issues, allowing developers to address issues proactively and enhance the overall quality of web applications.

8. Content Creation and Curation:

AI is increasingly involved in content creation, from generating blog posts to curating personalized content feeds. Natural language generation (NLG) algorithms can produce human-like content, saving time for developers and content creators while ensuring a consistent and engaging online presence.

9. Enhanced Cybersecurity:

AI plays a crucial role in fortifying web security. Machine learning algorithms can detect and respond to cyber threats in real-time, offering proactive protection against malicious activities such as DDoS attacks, data breaches, and other security vulnerabilities.

10. Dynamic Resource Allocation:

AI-driven systems can optimize resource allocation by analyzing web traffic patterns and adjusting server resources accordingly. This ensures optimal performance during peak periods, enhancing website responsiveness and user satisfaction.

Here are a few notable examples of AI Tools useful for web development.

GitHub Copilot: This powerful tool by OpenAI integrates seamlessly with popular code editors like Visual Studio Code and Sublime Text. It analyzes the code you're writing and suggests relevant completions, functions, and even entire lines of code based on the context. Think of it as a supercharged autocomplete feature that understands your coding intent and anticipates your needs.

Tabnine: Similar to Copilot, Tabnine offers AI-powered code completion, but it boasts a wider range of supported languages, including Python, JavaScript, Java, and Go. It also integrates with various IDEs and text editors, making it a versatile option for developers across different platforms.

Kite: This AI coding assistant focuses on helping developers understand existing code. It provides context-aware explanations of code snippets, identifies potential errors, and even suggests alternative implementations for improved efficiency. Imagine having a friendly coding companion who can explain complex code and offer helpful advice!

DeepCode: While not strictly a code generation tool, DeepCode utilizes AI to analyze your code and identify potential security vulnerabilities, bugs, and code smells. It acts as a vigilant guardian, ensuring your code is clean, secure, and maintainable.

The integration of AI into web development is not merely a trend but a paradigm shift, unlocking unprecedented possibilities. By leveraging the capabilities of AI, web developers can streamline workflows, enhance user experiences, and stay at the forefront of technological innovation. As AI continues to evolve, its symbiotic relationship with web development promises a future where creativity, efficiency, and user-centricity converge to shape the digital landscape. Embrace the power of AI, and propel your web development endeavors into a realm of limitless potential.

Free Tools for Web Development

Design and Prototyping:

- Figma: A browser-based collaborative design tool with powerful features for UI/UX design and prototyping.
- Adobe XD: Free for individuals, XD offers design and prototyping tools alongside collaboration features.
- Balsamiq Mockups: A rapid prototyping tool for creating quick and dirty wireframes and early mockups.
- Pencil Project: A lightweight and open-source prototyping tool, perfect for beginners.

Development and Coding:

- Visual Studio Code: A popular and open-source code editor with extensive extensions and plugins for various languages.
- Sublime Text: A customizable and efficient code editor with a large community and available plugins.

- Atom: Another open-source and community-driven code editor with a focus on hackability and customization.
- Brackets: A code editor focused on web development with built-in tools for preprocessors and live preview.

Testing and Debugging:

- Selenium: An open-source automation testing framework for web applications across various browsers.
- Postman: A popular tool for testing and monitoring APIs, useful for building and debugging web applications.
- DevTools: Built-in browser developer tools offer powerful debugging and performance analysis capabilities.
- Lighthouse: A Google Chrome extension that audits web pages for performance, accessibility, and best practices.

Version Control and Collaboration:

- Git: A widely used version control system for tracking code changes and collaborating with teams.
- GitHub: A popular web-based Git hosting platform with free plans for open-source projects and individual accounts.
- Bitbucket: Another Git hosting platform with free plans for personal projects and small teams.
- GitLab: An open-source Git hosting platform with additional features like issue tracking and project management.

Additional Resources:

- W3Schools: A comprehensive online resource for learning web development technologies like HTML, CSS, and JavaScript.
- Khan Academy: Offers free web development courses and tutorials for beginners and intermediate learners.
- FreeCodeCamp: A non-profit organization providing interactive web development tutorials and coding challenges.
- Mozilla Developer Network (MDN): A comprehensive and reliable resource for web development documentation and references.

This is just a selection of the many free tools available for web development. Remember, the best tools are the ones that fit your specific needs and workflow. Explore, experiment, and find the tools that empower you to build amazing web applications!

Conclusion

Thanks for reading this book. Share your feedback about this book by sending an email to rajamanickam.a@gmail.com. Remember, web development is not just a technical skill; it's a gateway to endless possibilities. You can choose to freelance and flex your coding muscles with diverse projects, build empires of your own with unique web applications, or harness the power of WordPress to create engaging content and attract loyal audiences. The key lies in finding your niche, honing your skills, and embracing continuous learning.

As technology evolves, the web development landscape will inevitably transform. But the core principles – creativity, problem-solving, and a passion for building meaningful digital experiences – will remain your compass. Keep exploring, keep experimenting, and keep pushing the boundaries of what's possible.

The tools and resources provided here are your launchpad, not your finish line. Remember, **the true earning potential lies not in the tools you use but in the value you create and the impact you leave on the digital world**. Go forth, unleash your inner web developer, and remember – in this ever-evolving ecosystem, the one who adapts, innovates, and delivers true value will always flourish.

So, whether you dream of freelance freedom, entrepreneurial ventures, or a career shaping the future of the web, remember – your journey starts now. Go build, innovate, and earn your place in the world of web development. The door to digital prosperity is open. Step through and claim your success!